West Cross

Westcross House
Bayview Villas
Baptist Chapel
Woodbine Cottage
Longfield
Ridgway Villa
Haroldmoor
Norton Villa
Norton
Alexandra Terrace
Norton Lodge
Bath House Hotel
Beaufort Arms
Elm Cottage
Norton House
Flagstaff
Oystermouth Castle (Ruins of)
Clements Row
Coltshill Quarries
Sunnybank
Oystermouth Tramway Station
Skating Rink
Castleton Terrace
Assembly Room
Marine Villa
Gospel Hall
Christadelphian Synagogue
Methodist Chapel (Wesleyan)
Claremont Villas
Sherfield Place
School
All Saints Church
Shortland House
Church Park
Police Station
Langland Villas
Glyn-cerrig
Rock Terrace
Troed-y-coed
Birchgrove
Ferncliff Terrace

Black Stones

Mumble

The Story of the Village of

MUMBLES

1   Oystermouth Castle and its doorkeeper, about 1870

Cover: Minature painting of Oystermouth and its castle, about 1860.
Endpapers, front and back: Sections from the 1878 Ordnance Survey
map   *All from Swansea Museum*

2 1850: the village by the shore

Swansea Museum

The Story of the Village of

MUMBLES

by Gerald Gabb, M.A.

1986
D. BROWN AND SONS, COWBRIDGE
in conjunction with
The Ostreme Community Association, Mumbles

DESIGNED AND PRINTED IN WALES BY
D. Brown and Sons Ltd., Cowbridge and Bridgend, Glamorgan

Contents

3 A wagon on what is now Castle road with the village in the background. Mid-nineteenth century

Introduction

Mumbles happens to have been the place to which a railway carried passengers regularly for the first time. Apart from that, the village which grew up on the narrow coastal strip at the foot of a striking grey headland is probably neither more nor less significant than most others. Yet it is full of interest. It had its own Roman villa (probably!), its medieval church and castle, its fleet of oyster dredgers, its quarrying industry, its pier, its lighthouse, lifeboat and coastguards . . . and even its own dialect.

This book is not full of original research. It aims to tell you a little about most aspects of Mumbles history in a straight-forward manner. The topics are in rough chronological order. Most of the information comes from after the year 1800, as the village grew enormously and people kept a better record of what was happening. The last section guides your steps along the streets of Mumbles, pointing out some of the history which is still around us.

You will find mistakes and some large gaps. If these irritate you into doing some of your own research, the booklist on page 75 may help. If you write down your own conclusions, better still!

In the following pages it may be confusing to see the names 'Mumbles' and 'Oystermouth' referring to the same village. Here is a little guidance. 'Oystermouth' is the name of the parish centred on the village, but once reaching as far as Caswell and Blackpill. Today the word is often used to describe the station square and a very small area around it! 'Mumbles' originally meant the headland with its twin islands. Nowadays, 'Mumbles' is a description of the whole area west of Blackpill of which you can read in the following pages—including the West Cross estate, the villages of Norton and Newton, and the bays of Langland and Caswell.

4 Mumbles, about 1865   *Swansea Museum*

7

Before Men could write

If you were to trek out into the middle of Swansea Bay at a very low tide, past the fishermen digging lugworm, you could find the remains of prehistoric trees. Objects like these are our only evidence. Imagine the scene if we were able to set up a time machine on the sea wall at Mumbles and set the dial back 20,000 years. The bay below us would have become a low lying forest, stretching across the channel to Devon and Somerset. Roaming through the trees might be bears, wolves, hyenas, deer, rhinoceros and mammoth. Their bones have been found in the caves of Gower, some of them around Mumbles.

A bone cave at the western end of Caswell Bay was excavated in 1832, but has since been destroyed by the sea. Another, at the Inner Sound, Mumbles Head was blown up by quarrymen in 1838, but not before elephant bones had been found. At Rotherslade Bay, below the Osborne Hotel, you can still see a bricked up cave entrance. When the hotel was being extended in 1891, work-men dug down into a 'V' shaped hole in the roof of this cave to make the foundations. All the rock and earth was tipped on to the beach, and among this debris experts afterwards found the bones of 16 Ice Age animals! A mammoth's tooth from the cave is on display at Swansea Museum; it measures 10 centi-metres across.

For the 3,000 years—think of it 3,000 years!—between the arrival of the first crop growers and the coming of the Romans, there is not much evidence. The museum has two well finished flint axe heads, one from Newton and one from an allotment on Mumbles hill. A lot of what we know about the first metal workers, the people of the Bronze Age, has been learnt from their tombs. A cairn from this period, just south of Glen Road in Norton was examined in 1969. Pieces of pottery and also the remains of a hut were found. The Bronze and Iron Ages seem to have been comparatively warlike, and on the cliffs above the Redcliffe flats at Caswell Bay are the ridged remnants of Redley Cliff Iron Age fort.

Roman Mumbles

Our ideas of Roman Wales are gradually being changed by the work of archaeologists. It used to be thought of as just a military zone, criss-crossed with roads and studded with forts, guarding the rich, peaceful lowlands of southern England. The Roman coast road through this area was certainly guarded by forts at Nidum (Neath) and Leucarum (Loughor), but excavations near the next legion base—Muridunum (Carmarthen)—show that even so far west they also built a town. So we should not be surprised to learn that there seems to have been a villa at Oystermouth.

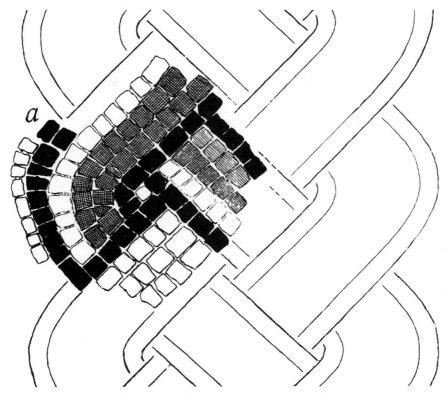

5   A drawing of some of the mosaic fragments by John Ward in
    Archaeologia Cambrensis, 1919   *Swansea Museum*

When the parish church of All Saints was being extended in 1860, workmen removing a bank of earth on the south side of the original building accidentally broke up a Roman tesselated pavement or mosaic floor. George Grant Francis, an amateur archaeologist who lived nearby, collected what he could, and you can see some of the black, grey, cream and red cubes of pottery displayed in the church today. Another clue could be the way in which the whole churchyard is raised above the level of the surrounding land; if you stand in the church carpark and look down on to Church Park lane, it is not hard to imagine yourself on the outer wall of a Roman settlement. So it looks as if a Roman or Romanised gentleman built himself a villa on our seashore. Swansea was not a Roman site except for a ford across the Tawe, but there could have been a track along the edge of the bay leading to Mumbles. On the other hand, links may have been purely by sea. This would mean a quay at Mumbles, which could lead on to other possibilities. A villa was usually a large farmstead, but it could be that this one depended on the sea. The owners of Chedworth villa in the Cotswolds are known to have eaten Bristol Channel oysters—perhaps from Mumbles? The length of Roman occupation at Mumbles is not known, but apart from pottery, coins from the first, second and third centuries have been found in the village.

9

The Parish Church of All Saints

In the fifth and sixth centuries A.D., after the Romans had left, missionary saints travelled through Wales preaching Christianity. St. David himself may have founded a monastery at Llangyfelach (near Morriston), and many of the Gower churches are dedicated to the Celtic saints who started them. Nothing written in these years has survived to tell us about Oystermouth, but later writers do mention 'Loyngarth' and 'Ystymllwynarth' as a place where a church was built at this time. The Roman building stone on site might have been useful! If this is true there has been a church on the site of All Saints for about 1,500 years.

The Normans arrived in Gower in about 1100 A.D., but our first evidence of their church at Oystermouth is dated 1141, when Maurice de Londres gave a present of the income of the church to St. Peter's Abbey, Gloucester. The document survives. If you approach the church from Mumbles Road, the medieval part of the building is at the back—the stone is a lighter grey. The tower and what is now the Lady chapel were built in the late thirteenth century, and it seems that even by this date times were not peaceful. Look at the narrow windows of the tower, its crenellations (battlements) and the way the walls slope outwards. The Anglo-Norman lords of Gower still expected to have to fight for their lives.

From the church carpark you can clearly see the medieval church on the left and the massive Victorian north aisle, built in 1860, on the right. Close your right eye and you are left with a typical Gower village church.

6 Print of Oystermouth church in 1850

Swansea Museum

Oystermouth Castle

The Norman invaders of Wales worked in small groups. About the year 1100 Henry Beaumont, Earl of Warwick, conquered the Welsh commot of Gwyr (Gower). He built his own castle on the banks of the Tawe and the town of Swansea grew up around it. The best land of the lordship was given to the earl's followers, and for more than two hundred years they and their descendants needed to protect themselves. They too built castles.

A castle at Oystermouth may have been built at once—and burnt down by the Welsh leader Gruffydd ap Rhys ap Tewdr in 1116. If it existed this would probably have been a wooden tower on an earth mound. Right through to the end of the thirteenth century it would have been little more than a stone keep with a rubble-work outer wall. By 1215 there was definitely a castle of Ystumllwynarth for Rhys ap Gruffydd's army to burn down. In 1256, Prince Llewelyn ap Gruffydd, who controlled most of Wales, destroyed it again. When Rhys ap Maredudd besieged the castle in 1287 it took him 17 days to capture it.

It looks as if there was more to burn down by this date. Edward I had stayed at the castle on 10th and 11th December, 1284 as guest of William de Breos, lord of Gower. From this time on the castle was generally owned by a lord like de Breos who did not often visit it. The last de Breos, Alina, probably lived at the castle at the time when its chapel was built. She married John de Mowbray, and the de Mowbrays were lords of Gower, including Oystermouth, until 1479, when William Herbert replaced them. (The Herberts became Earls of Worcester in 1514 and Dukes of Beaufort in 1682. In 1927 the Duke of Beaufort sold the castle to Swansea Corporation.)

Remember that the castle was not just a stronghold where the lord could find safety. He also used it as a centre from which taxes could be collected, service received and justice given. The manor court and prison in the castle were used until the middle of the seventeenth century. Remember too, that very little of the castle you see today was part of the building so often attacked in the middle ages. It is really a rather attractive residence built just a little later by the lords of Gower. If you look at the castle from the ridge overlooking the sea, the tower on the right, with the beautiful window, was the chapel tower, the most modern part of the castle. The gatehouse with the battlements and curtain walls either side of it are not much older. The curved recesses either side of the gate were meant for two large drum towers; their foundations were certainly laid, but whether the towers were built, nobody knows. If you walk through the gate, the chapel tower is ahead on the right, and the keep is just to its left. Try to imagine that keep standing quite alone and the rest of the castle growing up around it over many years.

The grassy field below the walls may once have been an outer courtyard with some sort of wall around it. During recent dry summers the outlines of two large medieval buildings have been traced in the dip near the castle. Could one of these have been the barn where tithes were collected, or is it too far from the church? It seems likely that the castle had its own quay near where the Savoy

7 The castle in about 1870. Notice the open doorway to the left of the gate where the round tower was sited

Swansea Museum

Restaurant is today—boats would have been easily the quickest link with the lord's castle at Swansea. In 1844 the castle field was known as 'Dove field' because it was the site of the castle's pigeon house. Pigeons were kept for winter food. You can still see the pigeon houses at Oxwich and Penrice castles, but the site of Oystermouth's was not rediscovered until 1968. It was in remarkably good repair when William Butler drew it in 1849 and in 1877 it was marked on the Ordnance Survey map. If you walk to the corner of the allotments on the sea side of the castle and then on up the slope you will pass very close to the site of the pigeon house, but there is nothing to see.

By the eighteenth century the castle was being used as a quarry for good dressed stone and a byre for cattle. Before the 1840s, when George Grant Francis supervised a program of repair work, it was in a very poor state. The City Council completed large scale renovations in 1985, and the castle is open to the public from Easter through to the end of September—why not go and people its rooms with your imagination?

8 The castle courtyard in about 1879. The charm of the castle, draped as it was with ivy, made it the subject of many nineteenth-century prints, drawings and photographs

Swansea Museum

The Villages of the Parish of Oystermouth

The parish church, then, inherited a Roman site. You might have expected the castle to be built nearby, but the Norman who built it must have realised the need for a site on a hill. So there was quite a gap between church and castle. Where was the village? It could be that the houses nestled under the castle walls. Or perhaps the settlement at the Dunns near the church had early beginnings. We have a little evidence from the sixteenth and seventeenth centuries.

In the 1690s Mr. Edward Lhuyd was putting together a geographical diction-ary of Wales. Most of his information came from local residents. His description of Oystermouth (in July, 1697) came from Isaac Hamon, a well educated Bishopston man, whose account is full of interest. South Gower is a place of "harbours and creeks where they do transport much limestones and other goods", and where "these sort of fish be taken . . . salmon, herring, suen, cod, mackrell, plais, millet, sole, flooke, flawnders, thornback, skate, whiting, turbut, hawk, congger-eeles, bowman, bream, and of shellfish, crabs, lobster, musles, cockles, oysters, etc. . . ." He gives us more light on the Roman villa:

"... part of the churchyard was formerly paved with small bricks like dices, but something larger, of divers colours as red, white, yellow, etc., which lies scattered abt. still. The people call it the Saints pavement. . . . The Sextons and others of late years have found in makeing graves many plates or pieces of the same pavement . . ."

He says quite a lot about the economy of the area:

"The southern pt. of this pish. (which is the larger) is Corn ground, mead and pasture, with store of limestones in and under it, the northern pt. thereof is colder lands and some good corn ground is there alsoe, the rest is woods and woody ground, and in the northern end of the pish is the forest of Clyne, where is great coale workes besides the veynes of coales there unwrought . . . In this parish is a safe harbour for ships as well on the sands or flats, as also in ye roade, here is two banks or Islands near the roade, commonly called ye outer mumble and the midle mumble . . . Here are boates imployed in & about ye takeing of oysters every year from the latter end of Augt. untill the beginning of May next following, in the weares (within this pish.) and otherwise they take divers sorts of fish. . . ."

The language of South Gower as a whole, he says, is a dialect of English. He gives a list of dialect words: 'horvie' (foul, dirty), 'knock' (a round hill), 'Leere' (empty), 'ven' (dirt), 'weest' (dismal), 'Tutt' (little heap of earth—the name still given to the little headland at Bracelet Bay on which the coastguard station stands). He gives forty six words in all, but states:

"The people that were born in Qu. Elizabeths time & dyed about 30 or 40 yeares agoe, used these words & some other words besides . . . (but they are) now out of use . . .", though a habit which still continued was pro-nouncing 'v' for 'f' and 'z' for 's'."

In passing Hamon also mentions wall paintings at the castle, Brockhole well which "(they say) is good for the eyes", "silver mines at ye Cliffe at Oystermouth" and two prehistoric stones called the Hoarstones standing in a cornfield. He sums up by saying that the parish has three large villages (probably Newton, Norton and Mumbles itself) and "the number of inhabitants are 110, of psons. Totally abt. 500". (Could 'inhabitants' mean 'householders'?)

The area he describes with its limestone and farms, its collieries in the Clyne valley, its oyster fishery and its dialect, was not turned upside down until our own century, when Mumbles was changed from a Gower village into a suburb of Swansea. And we can compare Mr. Hamon's fascinating picture with a shorter account dating from the 1580s, also recorded by Edward Lhuyd:

> "Ostermouth in Welsh ystyn Lloynarth a parish church not far hence stood a castle of yt. name.
>
> Quaere for ye building . . . (quarry?) . . . within yt. parish be some hamlets as bustleton, newton, hoxton, codeshill graing, (Coltshill grange?) and mayles (Mayals)."

But the most important sentence is . . .

> "within yt. parish is a common port or passage into England wherein is built a kay for that purpose".

It is not hard to picture the little trading vessels on the mud flats off Blackpill or Mumbles, perhaps floating with the high tide into the Horsepool which was opposite the bottom of Western lane. Mumbles was a seagoing village!

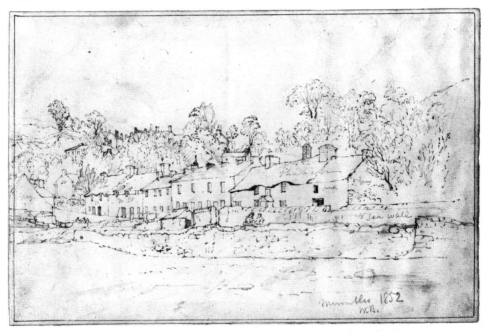

9 Drawing of Mumbles in 1852 by William Butler. It seems to be the cottages in the area of the 'Marine' leading to the bottom of Western lane, with 'Rosehill' (St. Anne's) in the trees above. Notice the thatched roofs at either end of the row

Swansea Museum

15

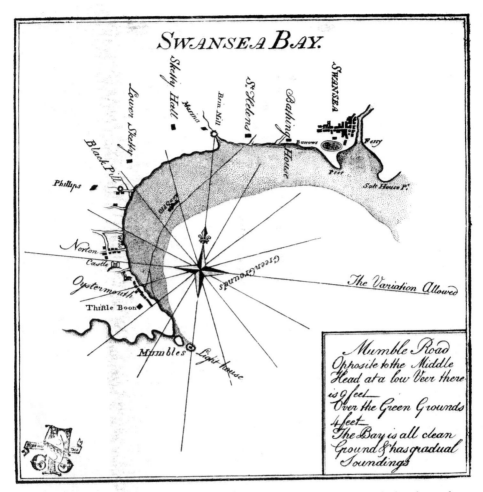

SWANSEA BAY.

Swansea

Shelly Hall

Lower Shelly

Marina

Brn Nill

St. Helena

Bathing House

Black Pill

Barrows

Ferry

Pees

Phillips

Salt House P.

Norton Castle

Oystermouth

Green Grounds

Soundings

The Variation Allowed

Thistle Boon

Mumbles   *Light house*

*Mumble Road
Opposite to the Middle
Head at a low Veer there
is 9 feet
Over the Green Grounds
4 feet
The Bay is all clean
Ground & has gradual
Soundings*

11 The bay in the 1790s, a map included in the tidetables of the time. The hamlets and
houses are well scattered. Marino was an octagonal house owned by Edward King
which is now part of Singleton Abbey. 'Phillips' refers to Richard Phillips who
owned 'Woodlands' or Clyne Castle. Notice the old quay opposite Blackpill
Swansea Museum

Mumbles in 1844

The most useful historical map of Mumbles is the tithe map of 1844. Tithes were originally one tenth of every thing produced on the land, which was given to the church. In 1836 an Act of Parliament laid down that tithes could no longer be paid in hay, corn, eggs, wool or livestock, but had to be in money. The amount depended on the area and use of each piece of land. So a detailed map of every parish had to be drawn, with lists giving particulars of every plot, building and field. There are earlier maps showing the area as well as prints, paintings and drawings of its features, but what is wonderful about the tithe map is that it shows the whole parish in great detail, and ties people to places.

The empty spaces are vast. Langland Bay is called Longland. It has just two houses, both near the present Langland Bay Hotel, the smaller called Longland House. William Phillips, who lived there, looked out over his four acres of fields to the beach, a view uncluttered by beach huts, carparks and tennis courts. (A surprisingly large amount of the cliffland was cultivated.) On the cliff between Langland and Caswell is just one house, David Loyd's 'Cliff Close', the ruins of which can still be seen in the middle of the golf course there. Caswell Bay has only one house, Caswell Bay Cottage, which despite its name was a large building on the site of today's carpark. It had been built by William Tucker of Horton in 1822, and by 1855 it was the rather grand country cottage of John Dillwyn Llewelyn, the pioneer photographer and squire of Penllergaer. He took some fine pictures of the nearby bay, and the census of 1851 shows five servants on the premises, even though only two very young Llewelyns were in residence. Between Caswell and Newton are only two buildings, and there must have been a lime kiln in the vicinity, because they are called 'Kiln Green' and 'Kiln Cottage'. The road they both stand on must have been a track, but it is very much the Caswell Road of today—three quarters of our important roads do follow the routes of these tracks of 1844.

The villages of Newton and Norton are well established. As today, Newton was a close packed huddle of houses and gardens on both sides of Newton Road and Nottage Road. There were a number of barns, including one at the junction of these two roads, and a large meadow alongside Nottage Road. John Woolacott was licensee of the 'Rock and Fountain', which had a two acre garden behind it. There were two other pubs—the 'Ship and Castle' on the site of today's Post Office and, confusingly, the 'Ship', a little further down Newton Road. Norton shows more evidence of quarrying, with a kiln and quarry marked behind Glen Road. The three large houses of the village had all been built—Norton Villa, Norton Lodge and Norton Hall (now Norton House)—and they gave employment to indoor and outdoor servants. Yet the work for most of these villagers must have been in the surrounding fields. Norton had only one pub, the 'Beaufort Arms', which still exists—though in 1830 you could have visited the 'Dove', and by 1854 there was the 'Cross Inn'. On the road which led from Norton behind the castle were Forge field and lime kilns field, though no buildings are marked. At the junction with Lime Kiln Road is a small house, very much on the site of the playground shelter of the Infants school.

The road from Newton to the Dunns has only two houses beside it, one near today's doctors' surgery at the junction with Langland Road, the other, 'Duns Cottage', is today's British Legion club. Further down, Daniel Taylor kept the 'Nag's Head' (now the 'Oystercatcher'), but the 'White Rose' was a private house owned by Mary Maddox Angell. Where the library is in Dunn's lane stood the British (nonconformist) school, with the Wesleyan chapel in front of it—though much smaller than the imposing building we see today. The parish church had a lodge on the main road and two cottages just beyond it—Rose Bank cottage and Shortland cottage. From these along the shore out towards the Head were the houses described as 'Mumbles Village'.

This village was made up of Western lane, Village lane, Thistleboon and the main road from Western lane to the point where houses petered out just beyond the George Hotel. Along the main road the landowner and landlord was the Duke of Beaufort, the lord of the manor. Opposite the bottom of Western lane lay the Horsepool and where the toilets are today stood a house. All the houses on the landward side of the road had gardens opposite, on the seashore, one with pigsties. Opposite the 'George' was the last of the houses owned by John Knight. (All these buildings on the sea side of the road were demolished in July, 1887, to make way for the promenade and, afterwards, the extension of the railway.) The 'George' was then the 'George and Dragon'— with about six houses beyond it and, surprisingly, only two beside it in Dickslade. The three storey house at the bottom of Dickslade was then the 'Beaufort Arms'. John Stephens kept the 'Mermaid'. The Conservative Club was the 'Ship and Castle'. The lower part of Western lane was dominated by what is now the St. Anne's hotel, then the residence of Henry Bath, a Swansea shipowner. He called it 'Rosehill'. At the top of the hill were the farmhouse, stables and barns of John and Thomas Nicholl, who also ran a pub with its own malthouse. Thistleboon House, which local people remember as an orphanage, had existed as early as 1790, being the residence of the Shewen family in the first years of the nineteenth century. In 1844 it was let in two parts—to Evan William and Thomas Bowen. The road from Thistleboon to Limeslade had only five buildings. Thomas Nicholl's brewhouse was one. On the bend stood 'Mear Pool' house leased by Sir John Morris—today's name is 'Mare's Pool' cottage. The map shows the pool on the opposite side of the road.

Back on the Swansea side of the Dunns (the bus station area), was, and is, a row of cottages called Clement's Row. Catherine Tetherley owned the free-hold of at least fifteen of these houses. She lived in a large house across the road, (which was afterwards called the'Elms') on the carpark site. She was a consider-able landowner in Dunns and Norton. The cottages were all leased to George Clement, and the quarry behind is known as Clement's quarry, but oddly enough none of the tenants as shown in the censuses of 1841 or 1851 was a quarryman. The Mumbles railway track is shown curving past the 'Elms' to end where our mini roundabout is today—a terminus convenient for transport-ing quarried limestone.

12 Oil painting by James Harris senior (1810-1887) on display in Swansea Museum. Painted about 1860, it shows, from left to right, All Saints Church, the two chapels mentioned below, and behind the buildings in the Dunns the large 'Marine Villa' (the British Legion). A boat's mast partly hides the road through the fields to the village of Newton on the crest of the hill

13 Print of the Dunns, about 1865. The nearer chapel was the Wesleyan chapel of the time, and next door but one is Mount Sion (1850). The empty patch of land jutting out into the sea was the site of Dun's mansion, the ruins having been demolished. On the far right is the 'Elms', with the Mumbles railway terminus just beyond it   *Oystermouth Historical Association*

A Plan

of

DUPPS

The Property of Mrs Sarah Angel

J. Morgan Surveyor

EXPLANATION

The Lease shaded Green is the Court Yard in Question with the Lime Road thereto in.

A Part of the Ale Well lett by the Lime Road
B A Gate
C The Front of an old Summer House
D The remains of an old Stile and Stile Yard
E Where stood a Landing Stile
F An Inner Court
G Where stairs formerly were
H Where a Gateway
I The Right descending to the Court Yard

SCALE

[map labels:]
Road to Merton
Mr Angeli D. Shown Land Esq's Land
Portsmouth to Swansea
Cambria Shop
Dwelling House Morris
Wet Road
The Public Path Dunn's Road
Cow House
Garden
Dwelling House
Garden
Cottage
Taylors Head Public House
Mr Taylor's Property
Cottage
Cottage
Bank of Earth
Cottage
Chapel
Tram Road

Dun's Mansion

In 1844 Mary Maddox Angell owned a house at the Dunns which she leased to Matthew Davies. In earlier times this was called Dun's mansion. In Swansea Museum are two plans of this house, which stood more or less where the bus station is today. The first plan dates from 1663, when, together with all the uncluttered fields around it, it was owned by a Mr. Madocks. With its barn, gardens and stables about it, it has the air of a very large farmhouse. The roads to Newton and to Swansea seem to follow today's routes, except that if Mr. Madocks mounted his horse at the 'leaping stock' shown, his way to Swansea seems to take him across the beach.

The second plan shows that by 1818 the mansion was owned by Sarah Angell, probably a descendant of Madocks. She rented out the house to a solicitor, John Jenkins. Outbuildings, garden and courtyard were all in a poor state. Mrs. Angell still owned fields in the area, but on the shore side of the road now stood the 'Nag's Head', some cottages and the first Wesleyan chapel. In a letter to the 'Cambrian' newspaper, Mrs. Angell claimed that her family had once owned great tracts of land " 'ere the sea had made its inroads on that flat which now forms the admired bay of Swansea".

A marvellous legend, still current locally, tells of a farm owned by the Angells in the area of the Green Grounds which are about two miles east of Mumbles Head, and of a path from Gower to Margam, all of which was flooded by a great tidal wave in 1607. No proper coastal road to Swansea was built until 1826, and the normal route was across the muddy beach; in February, 1804, one traveller was nearly drowned when his horse slipped into a deep pool. The sea must have advanced and retreated over this area over the centuries, and experts tell us that sea levels were especially high at the beginning of the seventeenth century. It is not hard to imagine the substantial farmhouse at Dunns with flat grazing land stretching out before it. As early as 1697, Isaac Hamon wrote:

> "The sea hath encroached upon a great part of the low grounds of this parish, as appears by the roots of trees, and whole trees that lyes in the sands, and other tokens . . ."

These were probably prehistoric trees, but that does not disprove a far more recent great flood—how great we cannot tell.

The Dun's mansion seems to have fallen slowly into ruins, to be demolished about the middle of the nineteenth century.

◀ 14   The plan of about 1818. It was probably drawn because the tramroad company had built a line across the front of the mansion—Mrs. Angell took them to court, successfully. The 'Nag's Head' is the 'Oystercatcher' today. The so-called public high road led across the beach. The chapel is the first Wesleyan building on the same site as today's   *Swansea Museum*

Changes

15 Two visitors look down on the village in about 1865. The nearest terrace of cottages is probably Dickslade   *Oystermouth Historical Association*

By the mid 1850s Mumbles was beginning to grow and change. Sam Ace and John Mathews were serving customers at the Pilot Inn, out beyond the George. The 'Greyhound' and the 'New Inn' (the 'Marine') were also open in what we call Southend, the 'Talbot' in Clement's Row refreshed the quarrymen, and the 'Albion' and 'Ship-a-ground' had also opened their doors. All of this was partly explained by a bigger holiday trade—there were at least eighteen lodging houses in the village, and Mrs. Hart had opened a temperance hotel with bathing machines and shower baths. As a characteristic industry grew eleven people described themselves as oyster dealers, though most, like Margaret Jones the postmistress and John Burt the grocer had other jobs as well. The number of shops had started to grow—four grocers, a butcher, three boot and shoe makers, a draper, a tailor and a baker by the name of William Pressdee. Such tradesmen probably made a living from the professional people who were coming to live in the neighbourhood: surgeons and accountants from Swansea, as well as gentry and retired servicemen. The village blacksmiths were George Clement and David Morgan, and the villagers included a haulier, a carter and a builder. Ten men described themselves as mariners, though many more must have made at least a part of their living from the sea, and Llewelyn Morgan had set up as a ship chandler. And in 1854 John Joseph Strick of Oystermouth described himself as a lime burner. . . .

Apartments to Let.—Furnished.

MUMBLES.

Bay View House, Southend, Mrs. Davies : 4 Rooms—1 Sitting and 3 Bedrooms

Castleton, Mrs. Clement : 6 Rooms—2 Sitting and 4 Bedrooms.

Castleton Cottage, Mrs. Parry : 4 Rooms—1 Sitting and 3 Bedrooms.

Castleton (Enfield Cottage), Mrs. Thomas : 3 Rooms—1 Sitting and 2 Bedrooms

Castleton-place (1), R. Baldwin : 3 Rooms—1 Sitting and 3 Bedrooms.

Castleton (Madeira House), Mrs. Harries : 7 Rooms—2 Sitting and 5 Bedrooms.

Caswell Bay (Horton Villa), J. Tucker : 13 Rooms—4 Sitting and 9 Bedrooms.

Caswell Road (Westbourne Villa), W. Blossom : 12 Rooms—4 Sitting and 8 Bedrooms.

Caswell Road (Park Villa), Mrs. Strecker : 11 Rooms—3 Sitting and 8 Bedrooms.

Claremont Villas, Mrs. Michael : 8 Rooms—2 Sitting and 6 Bedrooms.

Dorset House, Mrs. Hunt : 7 Rooms—2 Sitting and 5 Bedrooms.

Dumfries Villa, R. Davies : 3 Rooms—1 Sitting and 2 Bedrooms.

Fairfield Villa, William Morris : 13 Rooms—4 Sitting and 9 Bedrooms.

Langland Hill House, T. Grimshaw : 13 Rooms—4 Sitting and 9 Bedrooms.

16 From the *Excelsior Guide to Swansea and Mumbles*, by Charles Bath, 1880

Swansea Museum

Limestone

Walk along the promenade at Southend and look up at the massive rocky cliffs behind the pubs, hotels and houses. The limestone of South Gower is an important part of the scenery which attracts tourists to the area today. Once they gave a livelihood to quarrymen. In 1828, the Duke of Beaufort's agent caught two Mumbles men, John Davies and John Hullin, quarrying in a forbidden area. They pleaded with him, saying, "he might as well send them to Gaol as stop them from quarrying . . ." The Oystermouth Historical Association has traced a family of Beynons—in the early eighteenth century, Mathew, Fred and Henry were all stone quarriers, Henry (1760-1840) owned a small kiln to supply local farms with lime for fertiliser and his brother, Robert, kept a lighter for carrying limestone to Swansea, Baglan and Margam, in the mid nineteenth century, Cecil and Henry were stone masons, Robert (1883-1934) worked at the Mumbles Head quarry, and two of the next generation at the Norton Limeworks. All this stone was used for building and road making, it was involved in the smelting processes in the local works, and when burnt in kilns to make lime it could be used in lime-washing buildings or fertilising the fields. In addition, in 1808 Wallis and Gubbins set up a mill between Norton and West Cross where the stone was cut and polished to make 'marble' for fireplaces, tombstones, etc. By 1823, Messrs. H. Griffiths had taken over, and very prettily veined Mumbles marble was still available in 1860. As late as 1899 the old mill buildings were still standing.

A certain amount of quarrying must have gone on in the area from medieval times. In 1650 the lord of the manor was said to have a quarry on Mumbles Cliff worth £10 a year. By the early 1800s the main area of work was Mumbles Hill and the Head. Some of the stone was burnt in kilns nearby—the remains of two can be seen on the shore side of the Knab carpark. Lime could then be taken in boats to the farmers of the West Country, though the stone itself often made the journey. Limestone was also shipped to kilns on the banks of the Tawe in Swansea and to Neath and Baglan across the bay. The poet, Walter Savage Landor remembered "thousands of small vessels covered the bay, laden with lime . . ."

Halfway along the front at Southend is the Conservative club, with a very obvious quarry behind it; this was once the 'Ship and Castle'. In 1844 the licensee was Captain George Phillips and he signed a lease with the Duke of Beaufort which gave him the right to work quarries from the Knab rock right round to Bracelet bay. He then subleased the different areas to local quarrymen. By 1850 so much stone had been removed that the Swansea Harbour Trust set up a special inquiry to find out whether widening the sounds between the

◀ **17** An undated print showing at least one quarryman at work in Coltshill quarry behind the castle, overlooking today's Castle road. Notice the limekiln on the left. The artist has exaggerated all the slopes *Swansea Museum*

islands was destroying the sheltered anchorage for shipping in the bay. Captain Phillips told the inquiry:

"About 3,000 to 4,000 tons are quarried annually at the Mumbles. The limestone is valuable for lime-burning and is sent principally to Swansea, Neath, Port Talbot and the coast of Devon. I have rented the quarry since 1844. Quarrying has been going on at the Mumbles for centuries. There has been more activity displayed there of late in quarrying. About forty men are employed in the work. There are about twelve quarrying in the sound. There has been little carried away from the top of the hill for the last three years. . . . A man might shift about five or six tons a day by quarrying, but they are not quarrying all the year round. They are dressing the stone eight months in the year . . ."

It is easy to picture the quarried stone being rolled to the shoreline to be taken away by boat.

There were a number of inland quarries. One behind Glen road, Norton, was busy enough to have its own tramroad, probably an incline, which is shown on the 1878 Ordnance Survey map. The biggest was Coltshill Quarry which eventually formed a huge crater, and is now (1985) being developed for housing. The entrance was from Castle road, where the remains of a large kiln can still be seen, but there may once have been access from Newton road, near Underhill park, which was afterwards back-filled with debris. From 1920, the owners, Norton Limeworks Ltd., concentrated on making ashphalt for surfacing roads—during World War II they surfaced the runways at Fairwood airfield in Gower. Quarrying ended in the sixties and now the buildings have been removed and the workings 'landscaped'. Callencroft Quarry was on the

18   This rock arch was much threatened by quarrying, but finally fell to a storm in 1910. Print dated 1805   *Swansea Museum*

right hand side of the road from Mumbles to Newton, opposite Underhill park. In 1870 this area was described as "the entrance to a lovely glen, whose picturesqueness quarrymen are doing their best to destroy". Two impressive kilns lie hidden in the undergrowth, with the cart tracks by which they were loaded and unloaded still quite obvious. The whole area around today's cemetery shows signs of quarrying. At the top of Underhill park were more quarries, with a kiln in what is now the park woods. And there was quarrying at Langland beside the road to the golf club.

The quarry most people see today is Clement's Quarry, because it has been made into a carpark. Black lias limestone is found here, and it may well have been the source of stone for the castle. In modern times it seems to have been reopened in 1812, because hundreds of tons of limestone were carried by the Mumbles railway over the next few years.

Iron Ore

Remember the Beynons? Well, Mathew (1806-1885) was an iron ore miner. A vein of iron ore lay in the Mumbles Hill. Between 1845 and 1899 this was blasted out, broken up and barrowed to small ships, for taking to works in Swansea and Briton Ferry. This made a long narrow trench or cutting from a point just beyond the Bristol Channel Yacht Club right across to Limeslade bay. (Between 1931 and 1936 a large sewer and treatment works were built below Mumbles Hill and the trench was filled in with rubble, but it is still quite easy to see from the road or from the top of the hill.) The Libby family, who we shall meet again, were managers of the mine in the 1850s. In 1875 there seems to have been an 'ore yard' opposite the 'Pilot', and the Libby's forge was next to the yacht club site.

Just beyond Limeslade on the seaward side of the path to Langland was 'Doctor's Mine', a smaller deposit of iron ore. Boats would take the ore to ships anchored offshore.

None of the mining was on a large scale.

THE MUMBLES.

JOHN REES,
Family Grocer & Draper,
MUMBLES.
AGENT FOR W.&A.GILBEY,
Wine Importers & Distillers.

19 This seems to be an excursion on the railway in about 1870. The carriages have set out from the Dunns terminus which is in the background. The second is the type used for normal services

Swansea Museum

The Mumbles Railway

This line was built between 1804 and 1806 from the basin of the Swansea Canal (at the top of High street in Swansea) to a field on the shore opposite the castle in Oystermouth. It was supposed to carry Mumbles limestone to Swansea in waggons pulled by horses, and replace Walter Savage Landor's 'small vessels'. "That streak of black along the most beautiful coast in the universe", he called it, "detestable tramroad". The 'L' shaped tramplates were laid on blocks of limestone, not on wooden sleepers. The money came from a group of Swansea industrialists and businessmen. The company ran no services over the line; anybody could use it, hauling their own cargo in their own waggons, as long as they paid a toll. In 1812, William John was the 'cheque man' on duty at a gate near the Swansea end. The only other employee was a woman busy "cleaning sand from the plates" (rails)—the tramway ran along the shore. Her pay for 93 days was £4/13/– (£4-65p). Limestone, lime, corn, manure and coal from the Clyne valley, to which there was a tramroad branch, were the main cargoes.

Because the main quarries were well beyond the Dunns, the quantity of limestone carried was disappointing. In 1813 the company extended their line to these quarries through the unkempt garden of the Dun's mansion. Sarah Angell took them to court for trespass and the plates had to be lifted in about 1818. Very keen to earn money, they were all too ready to accept when Mr. Benjamin French offered £20 a year to run a passenger waggon on the line. So, on 25th March, 1807, he was allowed to begin the first regular railway passenger service in the world, probably using a converted limestone waggon, which was of course pulled by a horse. The service carried on until about 1825, run for its last twelve years by Simon Llewelyn, a Swansea auctioneer. By 1819 he used a rather more elegant converted road carriage. He probably finished when the turnpike road between Swansea and Mumbles was built in about 1826. The company had gone bankrupt as early as 1812, and from the 1820s to the 1850s the line was owned by the Morris family and continued to carry a little freight. In 1838 and 1846 great storms washed away sections of the line.

In 1855, George Byng Morris began to replace the tramplates with more up to date rails. He did not try to revive the limestone trade, but instead appointed a manager, Robert Williams, who ran a service of eight horse-drawn passenger carriages a day in each direction. Hardly any goods traffic is recorded. The trains were useful for professional men like the auctioneer, Robert Hancorne of 'Fern Cottage', Mumbles to travel to work. Mr. Williams also ran specials—in August, 1866, one brought people to a fête in Langland in aid of a new schoolroom. At Bank Holidays, thousands of people of all sorts came to Mumbles. After Whit Monday, 1867, it was reported: "the Mumbles retains its old popularity" with the railway using "every sort of vehicle from a carriage to a coal truck". Sunday school outings and Regatta day meant hundreds of passengers too. In the 1860s bigger railway companies tried to take over the line, but failed, and one unscrupulous railway builder called John Dickson actually laid an extension from the Dunns across the beach to the Head. But he had no proper permission and the new track had to be abandoned.

20 Train about to set out for Mumbles from the Rutland street terminus in the twenties. Victoria station (L.M.S.) is behind the wall on the right. Notice the bell on the locomotive for warning pedestrians

Steam locomotives came in 1877. The mayor of Swansea was very worried at this prospect, but there is no report of what Mumbles people thought as the first 0-6-0 tank engine puffed past Clement's Row and into the Dunns terminus. Between 1865 and 1899 there were long legal wrangles about who owned the line and who could run services on it. For two long spells the railway saw the ridiculous picture of steam trains and horse trams competing with each other. By the time all this was settled, the line had been properly extended. Sir John Jones Jenkins, who lived at the 'Grange' in West Cross, happened to be chairman of the Rhondda and Swansea Bay Railway Company. He wanted to build a proper deep water harbour at Mumbles Head and extend the railway to carry the goods. The Mumbles newspapers wrote of through trains of holiday-makers from the Rhondda, transatlantic liners calling at the pier, and the growth of a bustling port. The Oystermouth Local Board (see page 51), led by Nicholl Morgan a solicitor from 'Craig-y-mor' in Thistleboon, helped to push the scheme. Bridges or crossing places were to be provided at the Dunns, opposite Village lane, at the 'George' and the yacht club. The embankment across the bay on which the rails were laid ruined the laying up area used by the oyster skiffs, and the company had to promise two alternatives near the 'Ante-lope' and the yacht club. The Act was passed in 1889, but work was not complete until May, 1898. Lady Jenkins opened the pier, but it was never anything more than a pleasure pier.

The railway carried commuters, holidaymakers and thousands of daytrippers from Swansea. Once they had travelled three miles they were eligible for a Sunday drink in a pub. Three miles from Swansea's Rutland street terminus took you very conveniently to the 'Currant Tree' (the West Cross Inn), and a little further took you to the pubs of the Mumbles seafront. The 11 o'clock train home from the Dunns could be a lively affair!

From 1899 the services on the Mumbles Railway were provided by the Swansea Improvements and Tramways Company which ran the electric street trams in the town. In 1928 it was decided to electrify the Mumbles line. The steam trains went out with a series of minor accidents, the last in October when the 6.05 p.m. from the pier was derailed by the points for the coal sidings which were at Alexandra Terrace, Norton. One coach hit a coal truck and ended up on its side on the sea wall—but there were no casualties. An electricity sub-station had to be built at Blackpill. (It is the only relic of the line left today.) Work on the poles and overhead cables was well advanced when in a gale in November, 1928, two huge trees in the grounds of Norton House fell across them. Eleven large electric tramcars were bought, each seating 106 people. It was a fast and efficient service. The electrification was celebrated with fireworks and dancing at the pier on 18th April, 1929. When the weather turned nasty 15,000 people were cleared very quickly.

The railway earned a lot of money during the thirties, and reached its height during World War II. Its 150th anniversary was celebrated with enthusiasm in 1954. But the more fashionable use of car and bus transport gave the South Wales Transport Company grounds to close the line in 1960. Mumbles people did object, and today the decision to finish the railway does seem a big mistake, but moves to rebuild it have not gained enough support.

Mumbles Railway Society

21 Electric tramcar at Southend, 1959

22 The station square in the twenties. The people on the right have walked past Lowther's Pharmacy to a gate in the railings to catch their train. Those on the left are using the new motor buses

Swansea City Archives

23 Oystermouth Station on closure day, 5th January, 1960

Mumbles Railway Society

Oysters

When Rev. Francis Kilvert came to Mumbles in 1872, he ate a picnic lunch on Mumbles hill and saw:

> "the great fleet of oyster boats which had been dredging was coming in round the lighthouse point with every shade of white and amber sails gay in the afternoon sun as they ran each into their moorings under the shelter of the great harbour cliff. . . ."

The oyster trade was at its height.

As we have seen, Mumbles oysters may well have been eaten in Roman times. By 1684 the beds were called the best in Britain. In 1809 twenty-five boats were working from the village. These were large open boats with a single lug sail, but light enough to row if necessary. They kept within the bay. Tithes at this date were charged at £3·50p per year per boat. Jenkin Davies Berrington who lived at 'Woodlands' (Clyne Castle) sold the right to collect the tithes to a Mr. Knight, who, in September, 1857, tried to collect 10% of the oystermen's takings. He was drummed out of the village by the women, children and their brass kettle band.

The first larger vessels were ordered by Mumbles men in the 1850s. These were really cutters, but they were still known locally as skiffs. By 1871 there were about 170 of these boats, forty feet long, with fifteen foot bowsprits and forty foot masts. When not in use they were laid up along the shore between the 'Marine' and the Knab rock. Each skiff had a crew of three—master, man and boy. The dredges which scraped the oysters off the bottom were made to a special Mumbles design, many at Libby's forge. Each skiff had two dredges. The blade or 'sword' had to be sharpened regularly at the forge. The bag was up to four feet wide and a full dredge might weigh ten hundredweight. It was hauled up by a winch at the base of the mast. The two men would haul in the dredge while the boy steered the skiff with the current. Then the oysters were sorted into the hold and rubbish tipped back into the beds, and the boats returned to the beach. All the Mumbles oyster dealers leased perches from the Duke.

These were areas of beach where oysters ready for market (5 to 7 years old) could be kept fresh until needed. The tithe map shows perches off the Knab rock in 1844. Smaller oysters which could not pass through a two inch ring (a gauge) were placed in plantations, further out, where they could grow. The lines of stones which marked these plantations can still be seen in front of the rowing club house near the pier.

The industry reached its height in 1871 when 10 million oysters were landed, fetching £50,000. More than 600 people were employed, over 500 on the skiffs, 40 bagging the oysters and ten carrying them to Swansea, from where they

◀ 24 The ridge of pebbles shown here, used by the oystermen to shelter their boats, may well have been created as part of the ill-fated attempt to extend the railway to the Head in the 1860s   *Swansea Museum*

were sent all over the country by train. In 1883, the Oystermouth Local Board brought in a 2½ inch gauge, but overfishing gradually killed the industry. The only months in which dredging was illegal were May to August. By 1878 there were soup kitchens in the village for the victims of the slump. There were brief revivals, but a disease among the oysters almost finished the trade in 1920–1921.

Up until the 1880s, 1st September was the day of the bread and cheese fair, when the skiff owners treated their crews to bread, cheese and beer. Close inshore were punt races, swimming, diving and greasy pole competitions—the last along the bowsprit of a skiff. Children's competitions in building 'grottoes' went on far longer. A grotto was about a foot high, made of oyster shells, decorated with other shells and seaweed and with a lighted candle inside. Through the season, visitors to the village could buy their oysters from stalls along the seafront—as we buy chips in a bag. The better off might go into Lockband's restaurant in Beaufort buildings (near the 'Mermaid') which Gladstone visited in 1887—for oysters, bread, butter and tea.

Mumbles Lighthouse

25 Print of the lighthouse in 1814   *Swansea Museum*

To the south west of Mumbles Head is a sunken rocky ridge, against which sands build up. These are the dangerous Mixon sands. Off the outer island is another peril, the Cherry stone rock. Ships had to be warned of these hazards and beacon fires were probably lit on the outer head during the eighteenth century. In 1791 a Harbour Trust was set up to improve the port of Swansea, and one of their first moves was to build a lighthouse on the seaward island. By May, 1794 it was working. It was a two-tiered stone platform with two coal fires, one eighteen feet above the other. In 1799 the coal fire was replaced by an oil lamp which lit a large lantern with reflectors, and the lamp was gradually improved throughout the nineteenth century. Between 1816 and 1832 upkeep of the lighthouse cost £6,758 and wages for the keeper amounted to £943/18/ 8. This money was collected from ships which passed the light; ports as far afield as Pembroke and St. Ives in Cornwall collected the dues. Over these sixteen years £81 was taken at Bristol and £309 at Swansea.

In 1921 the Great Western Railway took over the Swansea docks and the lighthouse with them. Today it is run by Trinity House, and is automatic. When there were lighthouse keepers, they were Mumbles men. The second keeper, John Walker, was sacked in October, 1794 after leaving the light deserted for three stormy days and nights. For 75 years during the nineteenth century the keeper was called Abraham Ace (grandfather, father and son). In 1919 the keeper and his family were staunch Methodists. C. W. Slater wrote: "Of course they cannot come to (Bible) class or chapel, except at rare intervals, but it would do you good to see the class Leader picking his way across the sound when the tide is out in order to take the class ticket to his member."

The last keeper was Charlie Cottle, who finished in 1934. He lived on the mainland, wading or rowing across to the light, but when the weather was bad he could often be marooned there for a week at a time.

26   The original coal-burning lighthouse   *Swansea Museum*

39

The Battery and the Telegraph

The early plan of Dun's mansion shows a gun mounted in front of the house. Later a battery was placed on top of Mumbles hill—it is marked on the Tithe map. In 1860 a large limestone blockhouse was built near the lighthouse, to take two 10 inch shell guns. On the roof, behind a parapet, were three larger guns, 68 pounders, but for some years these were not fired for fear of bringing down the lighthouse with the vibrations. This was a time when an invasion by Napoleon III of France was expected, and forts were built near many bays and harbours. It was George Grant Francis who pushed for one at Mumbles. The Royal Artillery provided a sergeant and a guard who lived on the island—as late as 1883 there was still a resident artilleryman. The guns were regularly practised with by the 1st Glamorgan Artillery Volunteers whose commander was (not surprisingly) Colonel Grant Francis. In 1866 a reporter went with a small group of Volunteers to the island. He was impressed by the strength, orderliness and state of instant readiness of the fort, and by the way the gunners were able to shatter a cask moored far out in the bay. The commander rewarded his men with refreshments, including "the bottled ale of Messrs. Huxham and the meat pies of Mr. Fuller" which were much appreciated. The guns were able to swivel to cover an area from the Mixon to Swansea bay, and indeed a guide book of 1870 said:

> "The guns on top, working on a pivot, could shell the Mumbles road near Singleton, or burn Swansea . . ." (!!) though " 'tis true the guns would be utterly helpless in the presence of one of our powerful ironclads . . ."

By 1909 the authorities agreed with this opinion and had the guns pitched out into the sea to save the expense of moving them, but by the time of World War I, more modern guns must have been fitted, and the battery was once more manned. What is probably one of the original guns can be seen near Pockett's wharf in Swansea's marina.

Old photographs of the lighthouse often show the word "Telegraph" painted on one of the nearby buildings. S. G. Gamwell writing in 1880 explains:

> "Within the last twelve months the advantages of the national and inter-national telegraph system have been brought down to the water's edge at this spot, so that captains have only to signal with flags, or step ashore and write a message, and their arrival is known in a few moments to the owners and shippers, however far away. This is the only convenience of its kind in the Channel."

At the end of the century, the telegraph for Mumbles oystermen who ranged as far as Scotland in search of oysters was a marvellous means of reassuring their families.

The Lifeboat

From 1835 to 1866 a lifeboat was kept at Swansea, in the river at first, in the South Dock after 1859. Mumbles was a far better place to work from, a village full of men who knew the sea and much closer to the lethal Mixon sands. The Royal National Lifeboat Institution provided an open boat pulled by ten oars called the 'Martha and Ann' for the new station. The Duke of Beaufort gave land for a lifeboat-house, halfway between the last houses in Southend and the Mumbles Head. If you walk along the shoreside road which leads to the pier, you will see the boathouse on your right, with its R.N.L.I. badge still in place and its slipway on your left. No slipway could be built in 1865, because Dickson's extension of the Mumbles Railway had been made, on an embankment, right past the door. When the boat arrived in 1866 she had to be left on her carriage at the end of the village. Enough Mumbles oyster men volunteered to form a first crew and a reserve crew. The first coxswain was Jenkin Jenkins and the first secretary was Alfred Sterry who lived at 'Rosehill' in Western lane. The boats were given by fund raising committees in other towns, (e.g. 'Wolverhampton' I and II, 1866-1898), and by rich benefactors (e.g. 'Charlie Medland', 1905-1923). The men of the village gave the muscle power—the first boat with an engine arrived in 1924—and their unselfish bravery and maritime skill. In 1882 the Mumbles oyster skiffs themselves were hit by a gale when returning from fishing near Tenby. Three lost all their sails and began to drift, but the crews who reached the shore manned the lifeboat and returned to save them.

Many many times however, the crew put out to help large ships trading to the growing port of Swansea. Inevitably, on occasions the power and unpredictability of the sea has spelt disaster. In January, 1883, the 'Admiral Prinz Adalbert' was driven ashore on the lighthouse island and dismasted. The lifeboat went to her aid but was capsized three times by the huge seas around the islands. Much was made of the way Jessie and Margaret, daughters of the lighthouse keeper, Abraham Ace, with gunner Edward Hutchings, pulled two crewmen ashore. But Coxswain Jenkins lost two sons and a son-in-law, among the four drowned, and altogether four widows and fourteen orphaned children were left in the village. In February, 1903 the 'James Stevens' capsized near Port Talbot—coxswain, second coxswain and two crewmen were lost. And on 23rd April, 1947, the 'Edward, Prince of Wales' put out to the liberty ship 'Santampa' which was drifting ashore at Nash point, beyond Porthcawl. The following morning the upturned lifeboat and the three broken sections of the ship were found on the rocks. Both crews were lost. It came as a tremendous shock to the village.

In recent years large wrecks have mercifully been fewer. Tremendous skill was shown by Coxswain William Gammon in 1944 in taking the crew off a badly damaged Canadian frigate 'Cheboque' in wild seas. With the war on, two of the crew were over seventy. And it was Coxswain Gammon, of course, who was drowned three short years later. Perhaps a typical modern service occurred in 1963 when amid a chemical fire, which even spread flames to the surrounding sea, the crew of the steamer 'Kilo' were taken off. Since the first rescue of a pleasure boat in 1928, more and more calls of this sort have been received. In 1965 a very successful inflatable inshore rescue boat was provided by the R.N.L.I. The lifeboat itself is launched from a slipway built alongside the pier in 1916, the boathouse being added in 1922. Many local men have served the station for long spells. Jenkin Jenkins was coxswain from 1866 to 1892. In charge today (1985) is Derek Scott, who joined the crew in 1947, and became coxswain in 1955.

27 The lifeboat has always relied on the skilled seamanship of men like these. This early twentieth century postcard shows a scene 'at the groyn', a breakwater built by the railway company in the nineties to compensate the oystermen for the loss of their traditional lay-up for boats   *Mrs R. G. Lewis*

Paddle Steamers

Paddle steamers have come to Mumbles from the days when paddles were the conventional way of moving a steamship, to today when they are viewed with nostalgic affection. As early as 1823 a steam packet service between Swansea and Bristol was advertised, which "in the event of arrival at a state of tide inconvenient for entering harbour, passengers are landed at Oystermouth"—this was 75 years before the pier and must have been an uncomfortable trip at times. By the 1860s William Pockett was offering cruises to Ilfracombe and Clovelly with the "Temperance band in attendance". His headquarters was Pockett's wharf on the river side of Swansea's South Dock, but he also used Mumbles when necessary, and, by arrangement with Robert Williams offered free travel on the railway back to Swansea. When the pier was opened in 1898, Mumbles became a regular port of call, and Messrs. J. W. Pockett were in operation right up to 1914. 'Henry Southan', 'Prince of Wales' and 'Velindra' were all Pockett ships.

The firm which really put the pier landing stages to good use were P.&A. Campbell. The Campbell family ran their first steamers on the Clyde. They moved to Bristol in 1887 and started sailings to South Wales in 1891. P.&A. Campbell and Company Ltd. was formed in 1893 and soon sent steamers to compete in the resorts along the south coast of England. In the Bristol Channel they specialised in sailings to Weston-super-Mare, Clevedon, Minehead, Clovelly and especially Ilfracombe and Lundy island. They proved very successful, taking over rival companies and buildings ships of their own: 'Waverley',

28   A nineteenth-century print of the 'Velindra' passing a very exaggerated Mumbles Head. It comes from the cover of a piece of music by C. A. Emery, named after the vessel, and dedicated to Miss Pockett   *Swansea Museum*

'Ravenwood', 'Cambria', 'Devonia', 'Glen Usk', 'Barry', 'Glen Gower', 'Lady Moyra', 'Empress Queen', 'Bristol Queen' and 'Cardiff Queen' all visited Mumbles. Some of these vessels certainly lasted well—'Britannia' was the flagship of the White Funnel fleet (Campbells) from 1894 until she was retired in 1956. By 1921 there was no competition in the Channel. An example of prices in the thirties is: Ilfracome 6/6 (32½p), Lundy 10/6 (52½p), and Gower coast cruise 1/6 (7½p).

In 1948 seven paddle steamers were in service, but changing fashions in the way people enjoyed themselves meant shorter queues on Mumbles pier. Motoring and foreign travel gradually became popular. In the sixties, Campbells were taken over and the larger ships were slowly sold off. Smaller, screw driven vessels—'St. Trillo', 'Westward Ho' and 'Balmoral'—meant lower wage and fuel bills. By 1970 only 'Balmoral' was left, and in 1981 Campbells ended excursion sailings. Since then there have been sailings by other vessels—'Waverley' and the unlucky 'Prince Ivanhoe' which was lost in Port Eynon bay—but the full programmes of excursions which used to be a feature of village shop windows seem to have gone forever.

29 Captain Twomey, piermaster

Swansea City Archives

The Pier

If the pier never made Mumbles into a trading and industrial centre as some people hoped, it did make possible the regular visits by paddle steamers and it has always been a popular place with anglers. Between 1898 when it opened and 1938 it was owned by the Mumbles Railway and Pier Company. They were able to boost the railway by carrying trippers to the pier, and manager David James put energy and imagination into the entertainments provided at the pier pavilion and further down the boards themselves. At Bank Holiday, 1913, he laid on the Berlin Meister orchestra, the Ty Croes Prize band, the Society Idols Concert Party and, as usual, refreshments—"dainty afternoon teas a speciality". The variety was impressive—aquatic sports, musical competitions, a Jamaican choir in 1908. Military bands were a speciality; in August, 1906, the 19th Hussars band played to an audience of 4,000 people. The pier had a shop. Miss Martin rented the use of a tea kiosk. As early as 1905 'gramaphonic records' were in use, and by the following year 'sweetmeat vending machines' and electric shooting machines were in use. In August, 1913, the 'Mumbles Press' reported:

> "So tremendous was the rush for the Swansea bound trains from the Mumbles pier on Monday night, that one or two trains were compelled to go through the Oystermouth station without stopping."

So the crowds came. Captain Twomey was employed as piermaster; in 1914 his quarterly pay cheque amounted to £9/12/9.

In August, 1909, the pier brought the company a revenue of £493/10/11 and the pavilion an extra £165/18/9.

30 Illustrations from *Wright's Swansea and Mumbles Guide*, about 1904   *Swansea Museum*

31   From *Mumbles Railway Centenary Souvenir,*
1804-1904   *Swansea Museum*

After the war attempts were made to revive the pier's popularity, especially once the railway had been electrified in 1929. The format was largely the same, and results were only moderate. Times had changed and industry in Swansea no longer thrived. In March, 1938, the pier was taken over by the Amusement Equipment Co. Ltd.. Dodgems and games were introduced, over £10,000 being invested. Sunday opening started in 1939.

The Growth of Mumbles

The oyster trade was going well. The railway allowed people who worked in Swansea to live in Mumbles. Year by year more daytrippers and holidaymakers arrived, giving an income to shopkeepers and publicans. Mumbles grew. A census was taken every year from 1801 and the figures for the parish of Oystermouth were:

1801	715
1811	761
1821	1008
1831	1164
1841	1482
1851	1938
1861	2460
1871	3574
1881	3915
1891	4132

Isaac Hamon would have recognised the Mumbles of 1801, but ninety years saw big changes, and the twentieth century transformed the whole area. The area around the church sprouted the terrace of coastguard houses, the larger residences of Church Parks and Claremont Villas and the plainer rows of Park street and Gloucester place. A new locality called Castleton grew up above Dunn's cottage, later called Marine Villa, and now the British Legion club.

Oystermouth Castle & Village

32   The village in about 1865   *Swansea Museum*

47

The Congregational chapel was built in 1870. Beside it was Castleton house, for many years the bakery and shop of the Jones family, and now Covelli's fish and chip shop. Across the main road was Russell house and across Chapel street, Dorset house. Three-storey terraces strung themselves along the roadside, hiding the older, smaller houses of Castle street, Castle square and Castle road.

Meanwhile, the vast gaps on the tithe map were being dotted with the detached villas of the rich middle classes. Alfred Sterry, the first secretary of the lifeboat, moved to 'Danycoed' in what we would call West Cross or Lilliput. His successor, T. W. Islay Young, resided at 'Callencroft' on the road to Newton. Miss Strick's 'Brynfield' house overlooked Langland bay. (Today these three houses are a music and drama centre, a modern block of flats and a hotel, respectively.) The shops at the bottom of Newton road, which we tend to think of as the heart of the village, were built either side of World War I. Castleton spread up to what is now Oystermouth Primary school (built as the Board school in 1878) and to the Baptist chapel on the corner (1910). The width of Newton road around here gave this area the name of Broadway. Behind it, housing spread right up to Overland road, which was the old route from the church to Langland. Only the soggy fields which later became Underhill park blocked the spread of houses right up to Newton. The twenties saw the coming of rows of detached and semi-detached villas, like Caswell avenue and Caswell drive on the hill above that bay, Castle avenue in the centre of today's village, Bellevue, Riversdale and Moorside in roads in the fields beyond the village of Norton.

Since 1945 building has been on so large a scale that several of the original villages have been linked up. The council and private estates in West Cross now join the new housing at the top of Newton, which in turn links with the houses at the top of Caswell hill. The expensive houses of Higher lane, on the cliffs above Rotherslade, reach out to Thistleboon, which is now much larger, and creep down the hill towards Overland road. These new estates have surrounded the mansions of the rich, many of which have been converted into hotels or old people's homes, or knocked down to make way for luxury flats. By 1981 the population of Mumbles, Norton, West Cross, Caswell, Langland and Newton was 12,934.

Churches and Chapels

In the nineteenth century most people went to church or chapel, so more people meant more or larger places of worship. The parish church was first enlarged by Rev. Samuel Davies (vicar, 1821-1864). He had the north aisle built. He also built himself a large house near West Cross called the 'Grange', where, in 1851, his household included a parlour maid, cook, housemaid, kitchen maid and coachman. Under Rev. Secretan Jones a vestry and organ chamber were built (1867-1898). It is said that this vicar built himself the large house at the top of Newton known as the Manor house. In retirement he busied himself with recording local rainfall figures which the M.O.H. found very useful. During his long tenure (1898-1938) Archdeacon Harold Williams had the whole of the modern part of the church rebuilt. Newton people had no church of their own until St. Peter's was built in 1903-1904. It became a separate parish in 1933. Norton was granted its own corrugated iron mission room in 1908, one year after Graham Vivian, the self styled squire of Clyne had built himself a private chapel, which is now Clyne church. Clyne was linked with Holy Cross church on the West Cross estate to form the new parish of Llwynderw. A parish hall was built in Castle avenue in 1928, but this has now been leased by the community association as the Ostreme Centre. Church functions take place in the 'church rooms' in front of the church itself, a building which began life as a school.

33a and **33b**   *Overleaf*—Extending the Victoria Hall opposite the Wesleyan chapel in 1907. The second photograph incidentally shows the building in the background which housed the Oystermouth Council   *Mrs. Ida L. Puddy*

There were plenty of nonconformists in Mumbles. Their early meetings were in private houses or in chapel buildings much less impressive than those we see today. Paraclete in Newton opened in 1818 as one of Lady Barham's Calvinistic Methodist chapels, but became independent in 1822. The Wesleyan Methodists built a chapel on the corner of what is now Dunn's lane in 1814. The present one dates from 1878. Mount Sion in the Dunns started as a breakaway from the Westleyans, but has been Christadelphian for a hundred years. The Plymouth Brethren built themselves a chapel in Castleton in 1903. The Baptists have two chapels in the area—Bethany, West Cross, founded in 1850 and a larger church opposite Underhill park, built in 1910. The Congregational chapel in Chapel street dates from 1870. The Roman Catholic church, 'Our Lady Star of the Sea' is near the seafront promenade, and opened in 1919 in a building which had been Tom Owen's Pavilion.

This short list of dates says nothing of the religious life of the district, the self denial and tireless activity which raised the money for all these buildings, the simple piety of the people, and the central role of churches and chapels in local social life. In founding a mission hall at Southend in 1875 (now the site of the Irvine club), Thomas Gammon wrote:

"... the work is undertaken at the desire of a few believers in the Lord Jesus Christ, who wish to unite together for the worship of God..."

As late as the religious revival of 1904-1905 led by Evan Roberts of Loughor, there were very large prayer meetings in the village and many conversions.

The Oystermouth Local Board

In 1875 Benjamin Disraeli's government passed a Public Health Act, which led Oystermouth to elect its own Urban Sanitary Authority. It was responsible for the whole parish except Brynnau, which meant Mayals and Blackpill. Samuel Horman Fisher who then lived at 'Danycoed' came top of the poll, and among his eleven colleagues were a William Clement, a Thomas Gammon, William Burt the oyster merchant, and Richard Woolacott licensee of the 'Rock and Fountain' in Newton. Among the also-rans in the 1888 election were the vicar, David Secretan Jones, who had been chairman of the board, John Jones Jenkins of the 'Grange' and Graham Vivian, the millionaire squire of Clyne. Mumbles was not conservative in those days and most of the board members could be called progressive liberals; there was a strong feeling of independence bolstered by the strength of nonconformity. These men inherited a higgledy-piggledy dirty village and left a Mumbles we would find it easy to recognize today. It must have come as a great shock to people to find a medical officer of health, a surveyor, an inspector of nuisances and, worst of all, a rates collector among them. The board had offices on the site of our branch library in Dunn's lane. They set a rate of 1 shilling (5p) in the pound, which gave an income of less than £1,000 a year. One M.O.H., Dr. Jumeaux, resigned over his £18 a year salary—and all large schemes meant borrowing money. Fire fighting equipment was kept next door to the board offices, but there was no fire engine. In February, 1914, a fire started in W. H. Jones's grocer's shop and spread to the bank next door. Both were gutted before the Swansea fire engine arrived an hour later. A lifeguard was appointed at Langland and the board tried to make sure that ladies and gentlemen bathing there conducted themselves with propriety. The M.O.H. closed down the cemeteries at Newton (Paraclete), Oystermouth (All Saints) and West Cross (Bethany) and in 1882 opened a large new one at Callencroft. When the railway was extended to the pier, the board provided paths, crossings and a bridge to give access to the beach. They licensed the oyster boats and tried to stop overfishing of the beds.

In the 1880s the Mumbles road came to an end where the Bristol Channel Yacht club stands today. In 1887, the board proposed to demolish the houses on the seaward side of the road to make a promenade, and blast through the rock to make a road to Bracelet—all as a celebration of Queen Victoria's Jubilee. The Duke of Beaufort gave the land, and all was complete by the end of 1888. Adelina Patti, the famous opera singer who lived at 'Craig-y-nos' at the top of the Swansea Valley gave a railway truck full of ferns to plant beside the new road. The board gradually took over most of the roads in the area, including the main turnpike from the 'Currant Tree' (the West Cross Hotel) to the 'Beaufort Arms' at the bottom of Dickslade in Southend.

With its tiny income, the board had to be very careful over its plans for street lighting. The Swansea Gas Company laid the mains, but in 1879, for example, the board would not allow the lamps to be lit until October. In 1880 calico sheets were put over the lamps to stop them blowing out. The lamp lighters took a while to learn their trade. In 1883 John Kift was the lighter in Newton and N. Hoskin in Mumbles. The board was not satisfied and tried out Whittle's patent oil lamps and later paraffin lamps in Newton and Langland.

34   A gasplate outside the post office

Drawing by Su Gabb

Water supply was another problem. In 1875 the board ordered wells to be dug at the 'George', Village lane, Castleton, Church Park and Newton, but the first one was contaminated almost immediately. For proper piped water they turned to another private company, the Oystermouth Waterworks Company, which built a pumping engine at Caswell to propel spring water to Mumbles. In 1887 a windmill was built on the cliff above to help. Drought might reduce the supply to a couple of hours a day and, at first, only richer residents could afford to be connected. Larger houses might have their own well, often indoors. In 1884, Norton's only water supply came from two springs which flowed down from Boarspit farm, through meadows full of cattle, which are not particular "as to what they deposit in it" . . . commented the M.O.H. Some of the villagers relied on uncovered water butts.

Victorian Mumbles was attractive—from a distance. Some of the household rubbish was collected by David Eley who had a butcher's shop in the Dunns. All he did was to put offal, blood and refuse in a pit on the beach, so that when the tide was low and the sun was hot. . . . Nobody minded dumping rubbish along the shore and those drains that existed did not take sewage far out on to the beach. The M.O.H. often had to spread disinfectant to reduce what he called the 'stinks'. A Swansea man, a Mr. Pond, was landlord of two houses in Village lane which were especially filthy. They were built hard up against a bank on the top of which were privvies, with no obvious outlets. Both cottages were used to store rags, bones and rubbish, and, in one, lived a man, a woman, two boys and a donkey. The M.O.H. said he was "uncomfortable for days" after visiting a house in George Bank which was swarming with vermin. Animals were a problem too. Pig sties were often very close to houses. An early member of the board, Mr. Millward of Norton lodge, kept his pigs at the very bottom of his meadow, well away from his own fine house, but right up against the back of Alexandra terrace on the main road. In 1881 the M.O.H. inspected Thomas Mock's laver bread 'factory' in Newton. He considered the laver bread to be wholesome, but advised that the dung heaps of the neighbourhood be moved further away.

It is amazing that these conditions did not cause more serious disease. In 1880 there was one case of typhoid in the village, and two people died of smallpox, the second being Mathew Michael who had insisted on helping to put his mother in her coffin. Nor were the Michael family willing to have her bedding destroyed—it was too valuable. Yet neither of these awful diseases spread. Young children were at most risk—in 1876 eight of the fourteen people who died in the board area were less than one year old. Arthur Lloyd Jones, M.O.H. in 1900, put this tendency down to the ignorance of mothers. Once Mumbles people survived childhood, they often lived to a ripe old age. In the first quarter of 1881, nineteen people died; five were under fifteen months and five were over 75. Local people put it down to a healthy climate.

The local board became an Urban District Council in 1894, but in 1918 Mumbles voted to allow the Swansea Corporation to take over. Some local residents still rue the day.

35 A traditional viewpoint for the village is from above Clement's quarry

The following pages show three stages of development:

  a. About 1870—Beyond the trees on the left is the 'Elms', with its garden wall extending into the picture. The terrace on the seaward side of the Dunns is only half built. The nearer side of Newton Road is just fields, beside the wall of which the donkeys waited to take people to the bays. The garden of 'Marine Villa' (the British Legion) stretches down the other side of the road almost to the 'White Rose'   *Swansea Museum*

  b. About 1879—The shops at the Dunns are now complete—notice their canopies. The nearest one, which became Eley the butcher's, now has an outbuilding—a slaughterhouse? Notice the shape of the bay before the railway extension   *Swansea Museum*

  c. About 1908—A train is moving down the extended railway to the pier. The area behind the new track has been filled in and already used to build houses and the 'figure eight'. Eley's sign is now painted, and across the road the 'White Rose' has expanded and is partly half-timbered. The building which houses today's Midland Bank is in place and the shops on the far side of Newton Road have gone up   *Swansea City Archives*

Schools

Evidence on the schools of Mumbles is not easy to find. Here is a little information on some of them.

By 1844 there was a *British (nonconformist) school* on the site of our library. It seems to have continued until the 1870s—the Oystermouth Local Board took over the premises as offices in 1880. In 1860 the master was Mr. J. Orrin and sewing was supervised by a Mrs. Davis. The school was being enlarged at this time so that it could take more than the 95 then attending.

The building known today as the Church Rooms stands on the main road in front of All Saints. It was opened in 1856 as a *National (Anglican) school.* In 1860 the master was Mr. R. M. Bennet, and it is significant that he had then held the post for more than thirty years; this shows an Anglican school of some sort must have existed in the village by 1830. Anyway, in 1860, Mr. Bennet was in charge of 70 boys and 36 girls. On 6th June, 1867 a new National schoolroom was opened in a building in Southend which is now the Mumbles Motorboat and Fishing Club. The opening day saw a crowded special service in the church, with the grammar school choir in attendance and a train laid on for Swansea visitors. Harry Libby, who attended this school describes it as the 'Academy', but in 1907 he had to move to the new church school which had been built in Dunn's lane. This building became the village junior school after the war, and served as such until 1984, but today (1986) it stands empty. The church school log books still exist and there are some interesting entries—children absent collecting seaweed for the gardens, presumably after a rough tide, in 1900 and 1903, in 1906 the school was closed for a fortnight because of a measles epidemic, and for six weeks in 1918 because *all* of the staff had the virulent form of 'flu then so current. In 1878 the *Oystermouth Board school* at the top of Newton road opened. L. J. Bessent was head from its opening until November 1914. In 1903 it was renamed a Council school, in 1947 it became a Secondary Modern, and in 1970 a Junior Comprehensive—but the original name has stuck fast. By 1984, with all children over 11 being offered places in Bishop Gore Comprehensive in Sketty, the board school became Oystermouth Primary, catering for all local children below that age. At the time of writing (1986) some of the buildings around the original stone built main block are being removed, and the school may return to something like its 1900 appearance, surrounded by play areas and grass. The rooms behind the main block built for the infants in 1878 still house the infants in 1986. It should be remembered that the old parish now has primary schools at Newton, Whitestone (West Cross), Mayals and Grange (near Norton) as well. The old church school set up in Newton in 1863 is now the Old School House Restaurant and the new Newton school is on the hill above Oystermouth cemetery.

There have been dozens of private schools in the Mumbles area. The most distinguished was probably *Thistleboon House.* It was a private house in the early years of the century, owned by the Shewen family. It was offered for sale as a school or a boarding house in 1820, and by 1840 a school was in being. In 1845, the master was Edward Butler, who, in the 1851 census, was described as a

36 Outside the Dunns Lane school are:
Back row: T. Lamprey, L. Gwyn, L. Vaughan, ?, B. Michael, B. Ridgeway, ?, ?, E. Collis, ?
Middle row: T. Beynon, H. Gwyn, E. Chanter, P. Morse, ?, J. Bailey, D. Jones, ?, B. Dartnell, J. Kent
Front row: F. Murphy, G. Gosling, R. Furze, P. Jones, D. Michael, — Malloy, B. Malloy, T. Evans, ?

'literary teacher' from Tipperary. With his wife, Harriet and a young assistant he taught sixteen children at this date, some of them attended by their own servants. In 1859 the building was taken over by Rev. J. R. D. Colston who had previously run a school in Swansea, and who established a strong link with the Wesleyan church in the village. In 1866 an advert for the school said, "young gentlemen are carefully prepared for the universities, for the Civil Service and other Public examinations. . . ." In 1893 day boys paid 9-12 guineas a year and boarders 14-15 guineas, and the school comprised fourteen boys and seventeen girls.

Here are a few more references to private schools:

1854—Mrs. J. B. Bush's ladies seminary.

1860—Miss Thomas's seminary (possibly Bath house, Norton road).

1868—The Misses Mary and Ann Habbakuk's School for ladies at 'Har-oldsmoor' (between Norton and West Cross). Still there in 1876.

1870—Miss Champion's school for girls at Norton. Still there in 1875.

1879-1880—'Glyncerrig' (now the doctor's surgery in Newton road) was a school under Rev. E. Griffiths.

1888—Russell house (across the road above the police station) was a school.

1925—Bath house school, Norton.

In the early twenties there was a small convent school in Langland Road as well as St. Anne's in Western Lane. Mumbles Grammar School (head-master Mr. Davies) was 8/10 Langland Road.

If you stand in Underhill park, in the winter when the leaves have fallen, and look up towards the park woods, a house with a tower can be seen on the brow of the hill. Between the wars, this was Langland College, run by Miss Potts and later Mrs. Goddard. Uniforms were royal blue with red tassels on the caps. Miss Hammond took over later.

1929—Miss Brooke Gwynne's P.N.E.W. school—this was at first at the bottom end of Higher Lanes and later at 'Llwyn y mor' at the top of Caswell hill.

But it was the park which was surrounded by private schools. Where the hill steepens towards Newton is Brooklyn House, which between the wars was 'Westfa' school. Near the cemetery entrance was 'Ynyswern' (now a Spastics hostel) which was generally called 'Miss Pinkham's' after the lady who ran it. On the Langland road side was 'Clifflands' school; here is a 1946 advert for this establishment, but beware of the word 'comprehensive'—all of these schools were tiny in modern terms:

"Clifflands School, Langland, provides a comprehensive education on modern lines, and a comfortable and happy home for a limited number of boarders, who receive individual attention under the personal care of the Principal. The house, surrounded by a large garden, is situated, with no shelter from the sun, on high ground in a very healthy district. Girls of any age from four years, and small boys are taken. The Principal will be very pleased to receive parents by appointment to look over the school."

In 1949 Norton House became Norton College, not a school but "a residen-tial tutorial establishment" for a maximum of 12 students paying £70 a term.

Facilities by 1956 included a science laboratory, when there were students from Thailand, Malaya, Singapore, Hong Kong and Iran working towards university admission.

Mumbles at War

Both world wars had an impact on the area, not least by way of casualties. During World War I the battery on the Head was manned by Sergeant Foran and Bombardier Whiteford. The Wesleyan Victoria Hall was handed over to the Red Cross as a hospital. More than 500 wounded servicemen were treated, and many of them commented on the homely atmosphere. P.&.A. Campbell lost two paddle steamers to German mines in 1915. In 1940 their whole fleet of twelve was taken over. Five went down, including three off the Dunkirk beaches, from which White Funnel steamers rescued about 7,000 troops.

In September, 1939, a committee of five, including Canon Wilkinson (the vicar), Betty Howard and Harry Libby (a future mayor of Swansea) was formed to send regular duplicated letters to Mumbles servicemen abroad— 1,200 copies by 1945. The letters were cheery, gossipy and patriotic:

"Well, judging by the wireless there's a lot more rubble in Berlin than on the Ashleigh road tip . . ." (1943).

Mr. Libby's niece wrote:

"The purpose of the letters was to let the lads and lasses know that Mumbles is not forgetting them, to give them some brief news from the "Village Front" and as far as possible to keep each of the lads briefed with news of their pals overseas."

Betty Howard wrote to the women in the services and Harry Libby's spontaneous enthusiasm was very evident in most of the other letters. In the last one (15th August, 1945), he wrote:

"To see all the lights on around the bay and up on the higher reaches of Swansea has been a tonic: to realise that our Prisoners in Japan will soon be home is another: and to get basic petrol is a help even to we poorer folk who are glad to get a lift. . . . To realise that the war is over seems profound. Aye, war brought its trials. It also engendered in Mumbles a spirit of comradeship and brotherhood. Away went those little pockets of pre-war snobbery. We mustn't be pessimistic, but let's all be careful to ensure they do not return."

Looking Around

There is plenty of history around us if we know where to look and this section is a guide around some of the more interesting parts.

Around the Dunns

If you stand in the bus station you are on the site of Dun's mansion, which stood there from at least the seventeenth century until about 1860. The area where the buses stop was protected by a sea wall in 1818, and a new one was built when the railway was extended to the pier in the 1890s. The roadside lawns and flower beds are the site of a row of buildings erected in the 1870s and demolished in 1970 for road widening—the row included many interesting premises over that hundred years: Eley the butcher was on the Swansea end for many years, with his slaughter house behind the shop . . . the offices of the 'Mumbles Press' newspaper and the Oddfellows hall were in the middle, and opposite Dunn's lane was a large shop owned by Jenkins the ironmonger, which later became Forte's icecream parlour. Boot's the chemist was once Lowther's pharmacy.

The seashore carpark on the Swansea side of the bus station was the site of the 'Elms', which was built in about 1850, and over the years it was a private house, a hotel, railway refreshment rooms and offices. At the Swansea end of the building was the terminus shed of the Mumbles railway in the 1860s and 1870s. By 1878 a roller skating rink had been built there. And in the twentieth century this was the site of John Jones's dairy, which included a bottling plant. The whole area was cleared in the early 1960s.

Across the road is the entrance to Clement's Quarry (see page 29) which is also now a carpark, and beyond the Savoy Restaurant are the cottages of Clement's Row, built in the early nineteenth century. Where the roadside houses eventually peter out, you reach the outer wall of what were once the grounds of Norton House, which is now a hotel and restaurant.

Back at the bus station, look at the buildings across the Dunns, which is still the name given to the main road here. The 'White Rose' began life as a small private house a little way up Newton road. It had become a pub called the 'Rose' by the 1860s, and has gradually taken over nearby premises. The corner building (for many years this was known as Sanders corner) only became part of the pub in 1985. The 'Oystercatcher' was called the 'Nag's Head' until the 1970s, and has been a pub since at least 1818. The garage building was once Peachey's livery stables, and was probably converted from an earlier row of cottages. (In the station square opposite were Abel Vivian's livery stables.) Mount Sion is the oldest chapel building in the area, dating from 1850. (See page 50.)

Across Dunn's lane is the Wesleyan Methodist church, the third built on this site. Look for the foundation stone to the right of the door, laid by Sir John Jones Jenkins. On the wide pavement in front of the post office is a metal plate of the Swansea gas light company, dated 1869. When All Saints church moved its traditional evensong service from 3 p.m. to 6.30 in 1865, candles had to be used, but gas came to Mumbles in 1869, and was installed in the church by 1872/3. There are similar gas plates in the pavement opposite Underhill park at the top of Newton road.

A little way up Dunn's lane on the right is the Victoria Hall, built as a gospel

37 The Dunns in the sixties. The buildings on the right were demolished in 1970. The
reason is obvious, but the character of the area was completely changed

Swansea City Archives

hall in 1875/6, but owned by the Wesleyans since 1899. It was a hospital during World War I. The library across the road was the site of the British school (see page 20) until the 1870s, and then the Oystermouth council offices until 1918. The school just beyond opened as the National school in 1907, and served as the village junior school until 1984.

From All Saints through Southend to Limeslade

The most notable tombstone in the churchyard is that of Thomas Bowdler, who died at his house 'Rhyddings' in 1825. He owes his fame to having 'bowdlerised' the works of Shakespeare and Gibbon—taking out any references which might be unsuitable for family reading! The memorial to John Jenkins who died in the 1883 lifeboat disaster is by the porch, and a good look around the graves will certainly show you much else of interest. Three of the bells in All Saints once belonged to the Jesuit church of La Campania in Santiago, Chile. They seem to have been brought here by Aubrey Vivian after a fire burnt down that church in 1863, killing 2,000 people. (There was a strong link between the copper works of Swansea and the copper ore mines of Chile, and the Vivians were the leading works owners.) The church rooms on the corner of Church Park lane were built as a church school—look for the plaque high up on the gable. 'Beechmount cottage', 'the old farm' and 'Shortlands' on the other side of the lane are among the oldest houses in the village.

Until the extension of the railway in the 1890s the sea lapped up to the other side of the road opposite the church. But then the area behind the new railway embankment was filled in and on this were built the red brick houses of Devon and Cornwall place, Promenade terrace and the bowling green and tennis courts which were opened in 1921. On the beach opposite the end of what is now Cornwall place, nineteenth-century maps show a decided kink in the coastline, and perhaps a pool of seawater habitually formed here. The area was known as the Horsepool, and there are several photographs of oyster skiffs on the beach here. It could be that this was the natural harbour of the village right back to at least the sixteenth century. When the local board built the promenade in the 1880s, the Horsepool was filled with limestone fragments. At the end of Devon place is 'Our Lady Star of the Sea', the Roman Catholic church which was opened in 1919.

Back on the main road, the 'Marine' was called the 'New Inn' in 1875, and just a few years ago had a spell as 'La Parisienne'. A little further along on the right is Myrtle terrace, at the bottom of which is the Prince's fountain. It was put up to commemorate the wedding of Edward, Prince of Wales (later Edward VII) in 1863. The foundation stone was laid on 10th March, and on completion a year later 200 old people were treated to dinner and 700 children entertained in the fields opposite the 'White Rose'. A short way up Myrtle terrace is the old police station building—see if you can spot it! Immediately

38 The 'figure 8', which was opposite the church. Photograph from the *Official Guide to Mumbles and the Gower Coast*, about 1914   *Swansea Museum*

you come to the next right hand turn, Western lane, which leads to Thistleboon. A few yards up is St. Anne's hotel. This was 'Rosehill', the home of Henry Bath, the Swansea shipowner, and later of Alfred Sterry who did much to bring a lifeboat to Mumbles. In our century, the building was a school run by nuns. Back on the main road, notice the milestone by the Mumbles Rugby Club.

Carrying on along the front, you come to Village lane, which together with Western lane and the houses along the shore as far as the 'George' was known till at least the mid-nineteenth century as 'Mumbles village'. The next alley, though locally these are called 'drangways', leads up to the Mumbles Motorboat and fishing club. This building was a church school between 1867 and 1907, when it looked far more attractive and boasted a steeple. Later it was a meeting place for Swansea Little Theatre. The 'Carlton' private hotel was once a post office run by the Orrin family and later the Smiths. The Conservative club was the 'Ship and Castle' and is said to have been built by M. Maddox in 1737. In 1850 it was run by Captain George Phillips who held the lease of the Mumbles head quarries—the quarry behind the club building is still very evident. By 1860, the Misses Phillips were in charge and in 1876 it was Aaron Phillips. Alfred Hall wrote of the 'Ship and Castle' in 1899: "It was recently burnt to the ground and has been rebuilt." A little further on is the 'Mermaid'. In 1802 there was an old 'Mermaid' and a new 'Mermaid', licensees being Mrs. Stephens and Mrs. Phillips respectively, and as early as 1805 the old 'Mermaid' was "an old and well established public house".

When you reach Dickslade, the tall house on the main road at the bottom

64

39 Bowling past the 'Marine' in the twenties, with Western lane branching off on the
right
Swansea City Archives

was once the 'Beaufort Arms'—the publican in 1875 was George Bennet.
Notice the turnpike road boundary stone outside. The Swansea to Mumbles
turnpike was built about 1826, and this must have been its limit until the 'New
road' was constructed. The local board took over the care of the turnpike in
1884. The 'George' hotel was once the 'George and Dragon'. Mine host in 1854
was T. Townrow, in 1860 Mr. Joss and in 1876 Fred Birks. The licensee of the
'Pilot' in 1854 was Samuel Ace, who may well have been the pilot after whom
it was named. In 1875, Sarah Guy was in charge. The 'Treffgarne' hotel was the
home of yachtsmen before the Bristol Channel Yacht Club was built in 1902.
Just beyond this building is the site of Libby's forge (see page 29) and if you
walk about 100 yards along the roadside you will find the cut in the rocks above
you which is all that remains of the iron ore mine.

Cross to the new Knab rock carpark and the site of the oyster perches (see
page 37) is just out towards the head. On the shore side of the carpark are the
remains of two limekilns. If you take the road to the pier, which is the next left
turn, you will soon reach the old lifeboat house on your right with its badges
still in place, and over the sea wall you can look to the current lifeboat house
built beside the pier in 1922. The terminus of the Mumbles railway was just
short of the pier. From the pier, you can look across to the Inner Sound, where
the gap between the inner island and the mainland was adorned by a rock arch
on the landward side, much loved of artists and photographers. It was destroyed
by a storm in December, 1910.

40 The 'Mermaid' before extensive 'remodelling' about the turn of the century

Above the pier, the main road leads to Bracelet and Limeslade. It was built in 1887/8. A cutting had to be blasted through the rocks, and the contractor involved seems to have been James Dickson. For many years it was known as the 'New road' and it was expected that it would be continued from Limeslade around the cliffs to Langland and Caswell.

41 Drawing by Su Gabb

Up Newton road

If you stand by the Midland bank, opposite the mini roundabout in the middle of the village, you are exactly where donkeys used to be tethered in the late nineteenth century, ready to carry visitors to Langland and Caswell. The Newton road shops had not been built. Castleton Walk arcade, on the right hand side, is the site of the New Cinema, which opened on 26th June, 1927. By 1929, when the talkies first came to Mumbles, it was the Regent Cinema and, among other things it later became the Casino ballroom, the Showboat, Nutz, Tiffany's and Howard's. The arcade opened in 1983. Castle avenue which leads off to the right has the Ostreme Centre beside it. This was opened as a parish hall by Lady Bledisloe (daughter of Lord Glantawe) on 14th December, 1928, but it is now leased to the community association for thirty years.

On the left as you go up the hill is the red brick Castleton chapel, opened in 1903 by the Plymouth Brethren. Next door up is the British Legion club. This was built as a private house perhaps as early as the eighteenth century, and in the early nineteenth century the Montgomery family lived there. In 1844 it was called Dun's cottage, and by 1851 it was styled 'Marine villa', the house of William Meager, a Swansea shipbuilder. Other residents were: 1869 Leonard Williams, 1870-1874 Sir John Armine Morris, 1876 George Meager. Between the wars it was known as 'Glan-yr-onen'. Before the shops were built, its garden, full of large trees, stretched down to the 'White Rose'. As late as the 1920s the gateway was guarded by stone lions and the grounds stretched back to the roadside in Gower place.

The Congregational chapel on the corner of Chapel street was opened in January, 1871. This was the centre of a distinct locality called Castleton. The tall buildings of what used to be Castleton terrace, many of which are now shops and offices, were all built as houses with small gardens in front of them. The next turn on the left, Stanley street, was originally Rainbow terrace because of its bowed shape. The school on the right was built as the Oystermouth Board school in 1878 at a total cost, land included, of £2,500. The Baptist chapel on the corner was opened in 1910 on a site known as Pool close. If you turn right, the narrow lane is Limekiln road and it takes you past an old horse pound in the undergrowth on the left, and on to Castle road where a kiln of the Norton limeworks still stands beside the road.

Return to Newton road, literally the road to Newton village which you can now see on the hill in front of you. 'Glyncerrig' is the doctor's house on the corner and it is said to date from 1853. The Lloyd Jones family who own it have been doctors in Mumbles since Arthur Lloyd Jones was M.O.H. in the village at the time of the Oystermouth Urban District Council. Next door up is 'Hazelwood', built in 1892. This house had a separate office entrance because it was the Mumbles registry of births, marriages and deaths before Oystermouth became part of the Swansea authority in 1918. The older houses along this next stretch were certainly the residence of the rich. 'Ty Newydd' (No. 88) had five greenhouses and two of the newer houses now squeezed in between are converted coach houses. 'Ynyswern', built as a house, was Miss Pinkham's

42 The twenties—Newton Road by today's police station, shadowed by the trees in the garden of 'Marine Villa' (the British Legion) *Swansea City Archives*

school between the wars, and is now a Spastics hostel.

The road on the right called Coltshill drive was once a track leading to Coltshill farm, the ruins of which are on the hill above the quarry. Next right is the road to the cemetery. The cemetery lodge is older than the cemetery, and may once have been yet another coach house—at the back there is a stone horse trough and stables have been demolished. The first burial in the cemetery was of Alfred Gasson Gelderd of Waterloo House, on 18th March, 1883. If you follow the cemetery road you will see the overgrown remains of Callencroft quarry on your left—the area is now a nature reserve.

The next house on Newton road is called 'Parkview' and is a home of rest for the elderly. It was built in the 1860s by Hugh Morton Peel and named 'Sunnyside'. What is now the drive was once the cart track to the quarries behind, and it is said that Mr. Peel used the quarried stone to build his mansion and then declared that the blasting should stop for good. Miss Sybil Peel lived at 'Sunnyside' until the 1970s. The story also goes that H. M. Peel prevented building in what is now Underhill park in order to keep his view. In fact the whole area was very liable to flooding; skating on the frozen fields at Underhill was not unknown. When the Swansea Corporation bought $17\frac{1}{2}$ acres there to make a park, they spent £5,000 on the land and £1,870 on drainage work. Underhill Park opened in June 1925.

'Glynycoed', the next house on the right, constructed with huge blocks of dressed limestone, and with its magnificent trees, garden terraces and coach

43 Mr. W. J. S. (Jack) Jones drives out from the family bakehouse into Chapel Street,
    1926. The car is a Swift   *Su Gabb*

house, is the grandest in the road, perhaps in the parish. Charles Gold owned a
large wholesale grocery business, with an emphasis on tea. He came to the area
in about 1864, living at first in Myrtle cottage in Norton road. In about 1868 he
had 'Glynycoed' built, and gradually created its garden. He and his descendants
lived there until the house was sold in the 1980s. The coach house is to be
converted into a separate house (1986).

Opposite, and up a long drive, is 'Underhill House'. This drive once formed
part of a track which led to Langland corner. The house once had grounds
stretching right along the back of the park, with a large conservatory, an
orchard and nursery gardens. In the 1860s these were the Underhill nurseries of
Mr. W. White who also served refreshments to people walking to the bays. He
went bankrupt in 1864. The house was called the 'Willows' for a while, but has
now returned to its original name. 'Callencroft Court' flats across the road was
a house called 'Callencroft' until the seventies. In 1870 Mr. Ritchie, Governor
of the Glamorganshire Bank, lived there, and from 1875 it was the house of
George Islay Young.

Overleaf

44 Langland Bay in about 1879. Notice that Henry Crawshay's large residence,
    today's convalescent home, towards the right, is neither as big nor as ornate as
    it became—and it has a large walled garden. Look also at the unbroken skyline ▶
    behind it   *Swansea Museum*

45 Langland in the twenties *Swansea City Archives*

46 Redcliffe house on the western side of Caswell bay, now replaced with a block of flats *Swansea City Archives*

71

47 Langland corner in the twenties. The house behind the signpost belonged to the Lloyd Jones family, doctors in Mumbles for more than 90 years. The house has been demolished   *Swansea City Archives*

Down to Rotherslade and Langland Bays

John Jones Jenkins, who became Lord Glantawe, lived at Rotherslade in the 1860s. The ironmaster Crawshay Bailey also had a 'summer retreat' there in 1860. In 1870, the Osborne hotel which overlooks the bay was described as "Osborne Cottage ... the bathing box" of Messrs. Richardson the Swansea shipowners. Rotherslade bay was often called the 'Ladies bay'. The enormous structure which overshadows the bay is known locally as the 'White Elephant'. The Swansea corporation decided to build it in 1925 because the cliff was falling away under the path, the wooden steps to the bay needed replacing and the tea sheds were 'unsightly shanties'. Concrete was used instead of stone so that unskilled, unemployed men could be used.

The enormous towered building which dominates Langland bay in a far more pleasant way is now the Club Union Convalescent Home. It seems to have been built in about 1860 by Henry Crawshay of the Merthyr family of ironmasters. In 1866 his wife Eliza organised a fete in the grounds to raise funds for the new church school in Mumbles, and the Cyfarthfa silver band came down for the occasion. In 1873 Henry gave All Saints Church a new organ. In 1888 his house at Langland was bought by a syndicate as a hotel.

And down to Caswell Bay

At the top of Caswell hill is 'Havergal', a house named after Frances Ridley Havergal, the hymnwriter, who spent her last years there, 1878-1879. A plaque on the garden wall commemorates her. Near the bottom of the hill, just beyond the first carpark, is a coach house; this is all that remains of Caswell Cottage, a large house which once stood at the entrance to Caswell valley, where the main beach carpark now is (see page 18). By 1902 it was an Industrial Home for children, and it later became a boarding house. The Caswell Bay Hotel was built some time soon before 1860 by William Jordan and run by his sister, then a spinster. By 1875 she had become Mrs. Amy Langdale. Near the point on the western side of the bay is what is left of the concrete pumping station built by the Oystermouth Waterworks Company, and on the clifftop, a little to seaward stood their windmill (see page 52). The windmill was out of use by 1900 and after a fire about 1930 it had to be demolished.

48   Caswell Bay, about 1865   *Swansea Museum*

49 A selection of advertisements from a Mumbles guidebook of 1908 (given to Oystermouth Historical Association by Mona Michael). Baldwin's today is the D.I.Y. shop of the late Mr. David Cope, opposite the primary school. For some years it was known as the Star Supply Stores. Peachey's is now the garage in the Dunns. Varley's is still owned by Mr. John Varley

74

If you want to find out more . . .

What follows is a list of books, articles, etc. which I have found valuable, mainly by people who have done original research. Most of them can still be bought or are available from libraries. The Oystermouth Branch library has a small collection of local books and pamphlets, including copies of the 'Letters to the Forces' (see page 60). Among the useful material at the West Glamorgan Reference Library in Alexandra road, Swansea are the series of Mumbles newspapers:

'The Mumbles Chronicle', 1887–1890.
'The Mumbles Observer', 1889–1890.
'The Mumbles Press', 1903–1933.

★ ★

General

Norman Lewis Thomas: 'Of Swansea West: the Mumbles—Past and Present'. (Gomer, 1978)—a very full work of reference.

Harry Libby: 'The mixture: Mumbles and Harry Libby'. (1964)—very personal, full of life.

Prehistory

J. G. Rutter: 'Prehistoric Gower'. (Swansea, 1948).

H. N. Savory: 'A forgotten round cairn at Newton', in 'Gower', 1969.

All Saints Church

E. I. E. Phillips: 'Guide to All Saints, the Parish Church of Oystermouth'. (1961)

Oystermouth Castle

Much of the information in this section has been culled from the expertise of Miss Freda Marrison, Mr. Bernard Morris and Mr. Ken Lightfoot who is currently writing a new guidebook and has compiled the leaflets on sale at the castle. (1986)

Dun's Mansion

Bernard Morris: 'The drowned lands of Swansea Bay', in 'Gower', 1964.

Frank Llewelyn Jones: 'The way from Oystermouth Village to Swansea Town, circa 1800', in 'Gower', 1979.

Gerald Gabb: 'A temporary extension of the Mumbles Railway', in 'Gower', 1978.

Iron Ore

Arthur Davies: 'Iron ore mining at Mumbles and Langland districts 1845–1899', in 'Gower', 1959.

The Mumbles Railway

Charles Lee: 'The Swansea and Mumbles Railway', (Oakwood, 1977).

Rob Gittins: 'Rock and roll to paradise, the history of the Mumbles Railway', (Gomer, 1982).

Gerald Gabb: 'A second extension of the Mumbles Railway' in 'Gower', 1980.

Oysters

P. E. King & A. Osborn: 'Oyster dredging' in 'Gower', 1969.

Carl Smith: 'A history of the Mumbles oyster industry', in the 'Mumbles and Gower news'.

Mumbles Lighthouse

W. H. Jones: 'History of the port of Swansea', (Spurrell, 1922)—Chapter 18.

The Lifeboat

Carl Smith: 'The men of Mumbles Head: the story of the Mumbles lifeboat from 1832', (Gomer, 1977).

Paddle Steamers

Frank Jones: 'The White Funnels', (Newton Church magazine).

Iain Hope: 'The Campbells of Kilmuin', (Aggregate publications, Renfrewshire).

Churches and Chapels

Megan and R. O. Roberts: 'Two centuries of Mumbles Methodism', (1977). This is quite excellent.

'Castleton Chapel, Mumbles, 1881-1981'. (1981).

T. Bryn Richards: 'The origin and history of Tabernacle Congregational Church, Mumbles', (1970).

R. Barnes: 'The church in the lane: Bethany Baptist Centenary, 1867-1967'.

The Oystermouth Local Board

The whole of this section is based on the unpublished researches of Mrs. Brenda Masterman in the Swansea City Archives.

Schools

K. H. Bailey: 'Oystermouth School Centenary, 1878-1978'.

Museums

Apart from items mentioned in the text, Swansea Museum which is in Victoria road, Swansea, near the Leisure Centre, has on display a model of an oyster dredger and a number of items relating to the Mumbles railway.

Swansea Maritime and Industrial Museum has a larger Mumbles Railway display, including a tramcar cab, a pantograph and some seats. On the first floor are the original lantern from the lighthouse and a Mumbles oyster dredge. (1986)

Acknowledgements

Thanks are due to very many people including Miss Betty Nelmes, Carl Smith, Frank Jones, Michael Isaac, Michael Gibbs, Ivor Phillips, Miss Freda Marrison, Mervyn Owen, Mrs. Brenda Masterman, Bernard Morris, Ken Lightfoot, Ken Reeves, David Hawkins, Luke Toft, Mrs. Wendy Cope, R. O. Roberts, W. C. Rogers, Alan Williams (headmaster of Oystermouth Primary school), Mrs. Fona Beynon, and Mrs. W. G. S. Smith (my mother-in-law). I am specially grateful for access to the rich collections of "*Swansea Museum*".

The Oystermouth Historical Association holds regular meetings, owns a small library and archive, and puts on a regular summer exhibition—all at the Ostreme hall, Castle avenue. I have learnt most by just talking to people at these exhibitions.

50   Oystermouth and its castle, 1850   *Swansea Museum*

51 The shore at the Dunns, 1850, with All Saints Church in the background

Index

*Major references shown in **bold** type*